DRAWINGS AND SKETCHES
of
OXFORD

by William Bird

With a commentary by Jonathan Keates

THE SALAMANDER PRESS, EDINBURGH

British Library Catologuing in Publication Data
Bird, William
Drawings and sketches of Oxford.
1. Oxford (Oxfordshire) – Pictorial works
I. Title   II. Keates, Jonathan
914.25 740222   DA690.098
ISBN 0–907540–31–7

First published 1983

Published by The Salamander Press, 34 Shandwick Place, Edinburgh EH2 4RT

Printed in Great Britain by Jolly & Barber Ltd, Rugby
Bound by Hunter & Foulis Ltd, Edinburgh

DRAWINGS & SKETCHES
OF OXFORD

Merton

Cricketers and cows on Christ Church meadow take on the roles assigned to them by the landscape painters and garden architects of the eighteenth century, that of a decorative indicator in the scale of a handsome prospect – the handsomest, say some, in all Oxford. Yet there have always been those who would be happy to destroy it, driving a bypass along its river margin or scattering terraces and crescents into the fields.

Safe, for the time being, it remains, preserving that peculiarly English illusion that a city was never really intended here at all, and that the sudden presence of three colleges beyond the trees is a mere act of fantastic chance. It is Christ Church's in name alone, belonging as much to Corpus, whose sober Fellows' Building of 1712 fronts it on the north-west, and even more to Merton, lying right along its northern edge. Presumptuous Christ Church, discreet Corpus, and Merton, reposed in an absolute supremacy, just as it should be.

For the college, oldest in the university, has never needed to assert itself. Founded in 1264 by Henry III's High Chancellor Walter de Merton, it maintained from the first a dignified bookish reserve without ever forfeiting that enchantment essential to the Oxford experience. Thus its chapel is an eternally incomplete vision, the choir, transepts and tower of a Gothic priory, closed off by *trompe-l'oeil* panels on either side of the organ loft. Typically, while during the Civil War the fellows welcomed Queen Henrietta Maria, and constructed a special sunken passageway among the siege works and defences thrown up against Roundhead attack so that she could visit her husband King Charles in Christ Church without danger, the warden Dr William Harvey was busy with his pioneering studies of animal foetus and embryo. Quite as typically, his successor Dr Goddard not only created a panacea derived from raw silk, but enriched everyone's lives by inventing rum at Merton – a worthy counterpart to Dr Nowell of Brasenose, who found out the secret of bottling beer.

Merton can never quite suppress a tendency towards the bizarre and quixotic. In the squat, dark little Mob Quad, oldest in Oxford, Duns Scotus, greatest of philosophical Franciscans, is said to have transcribed the Bible without taking any food and (not unnaturally) to have collapsed at the end of it. This was, besides, the college which fostered the uncompromising dilettantism of Max Beerbohm, at the close of whose *Zuleika Dobson* the entire undergraduate body flings itself into the river in despairing adoration of the heroine. Wise, inscrutable, silent and very old, Merton, mingling the airs of a Zen garden and a mediaeval *hortus conclusus*, accommodates these things.

Christ Church

Jane Austen characterized one of her heroines as a girl 'clever, handsome, rich' who 'seemed to unite all the blessings of existence'. Christ Church would probably reject the 'seemed' though in every other respect acknowledge the similarity. It is not only clever, handsome and rich but also, more strikingly, enormous, everything about its opulence of proportion calculated to inspire awe in the visitor and to humble those other colleges which are older and whose undergraduates and pedagogues are, well, yes, maybe a little more hard working.

Grandly conceived and grandly executed, with a head called the Dean and fellows called Students, the House (its Latin title is Aedes Christi, the House of Christ – somehow it would be) disdains to call itself a college. Its gateway is a Wren tower like a Russian monastery, its front quad, called Tom after the great bell which rings each night to call scholars home, would have been the largest cloister in the world if it had ever been finished, and its chapel is no less than Oxford Cathedral, ensconced at Tom's eastern end and holding the shrine of St Frideswide, the city's patron and (some say) founder. Its coat of arms is topped by a cardinal's hat to perpetuate the memory of its creator Thomas Wolsey, but its patron is the reigning sovereign of England, since the college was founded anew by Wolsey's one-time master Henry VIII, whose obesity somehow suits the Christ Church scale of things.

Traditionally a nursery of Lords and princes (in Peckwater Quad, opposite a library as big as a country house and looking rather like one) it has also, at one period or another, nourished the soldier-poet Philip Sidney, the philosopher John Locke, expelled from his studentship by royal command for 'factious and disloyall behaviour', John Ruskin, whose aesthetic was to condition an entire Oxford generation, and W. H. Auden, a son of the House who found a rather melancholy refuge here in his final years.

As for its Deans – Atterbury, the Jacobite firebrand, met by an escort of four hundred horsemen when he entered Oxford to stir up sedition; Aldrich, architect and musician, friend of Wren and Purcell; Gaisford, most brilliant and magisterial of early Victorian classicists – none is more famous than Henry Liddell. Not for his great Greek Lexicon, which he worked on with Scott, the Master of Balliol, but for being, simply, the father of Alice. For it was here in Christ Church that C. L. Dodgson, fellow and tutor in mathematics, transmuted his secret longing and donnish conundrums as Lewis Caroll into *Alice in Wonderland* and *Through The Looking Glass*.

Folly Bridge

Oxford arose, like Venus Anadyomene or Britannia, from the waters, and will doubtless go back to them. Folk etymology says that St Frideswide, riding down into this foggy, rheumatic flood-plain mounted upon a cow, cried 'Ox, go forth!' and crossed a ford in the shallow, gravelly curve of the Thames to set up her house of holy ladies which later became Christ Church. Another tale, as respectable as that which attributes the founding of University College to King Alfred, burnt cakes and all, says that a band of Athenian scholars in the days of King Brutus the Trojan brought learning down the river from Cricklade ('Greeklade' of course). Weedy, misty, vague and somehow most Oxonian in their hankering after romance never wholly achieved and faintly tinged with comedy, these legends yet hold something true, for if city and university had any beginnings it was here at the water's edge.

The place perpetually remembers its origins on the mesopotamia of Isis and Cherwell, among weirs, cuts and canals, and little alder-fringed backwaters running to nowhere in a damp, glistening greenness. Amphibious Oxonians endure the sodden, bronchial, arthritic climate in the strange consciousness of a need to stay close to springs and sources which have nothing whatever to do with references to the Bodleian catalogue. Even in winter the dank Iffley fields echo with the formless shouts of an eight's coach, and the rowers themselves, fed by their colleges like champion beasts, take on the quality of heroic victims, cast upon the summer river in the ultimate fervours of Eights Week.

These are for the Isis (the Thames at Oxford becomes an Egyptian mother goddess). Punts, descendants, perhaps, of those 'ridiculous gundilows' the Doge of Venice presented to Charles II, inhabit the quieter, more dozily seductive Cherwell, poled from the sloped stern end (Cambridge takes the more perilous bow) and unsinkable enough to accommodate the essential postures of picnics, study and love. The two streams modestly join a little beyond Folly Bridge, named not for the fancies of Frideswide or the Cricklade Athenians, nor for the wizardry of Roger Bacon, the Franciscan magus who kept his laboratory in King Stephen's old lookout tower close by, but for the caprices of a Mr Welcome who repaired it in Cromwellian days. As one eighteenth-century undergraduate wrote:

> Near Welcome's Folly let me ply the oar,
> Where Isis laves, irriguous, flowry meads
> Or Cherwell, gentler sister, willow-fringed
> Her oozy banks explores, ere college bells
> Recall me to my book. Fair streams, adieu!

The Sheldonian Theatre

Oxford needs a theatre for its rites and ceremonies. The swank and flamboyance, the sense of large, extravagant gesture, often in vain but always imaginative, which burn themselves into its children, want a setting to sanctify them, and get it memorably in the Sheldonian. In 1664 the diarist John Evelyn, visiting his old university, admired 'the new Theatre, now building at an exceeding and royal expense by the Lord Archbishop of Canterbury' Dr Gilbert Sheldon, whose £25,000 was designed to transport the flim-flam and knockabout of the annual 'Act' from St Mary's to a more appropriate setting. The architect, Evelyn noted, was 'that incomparable genius, my worthy friend Dr Christopher Wren, who showed me the model, not disdaining my advice in some particulars'.

A young man's work, then, by the thirty-year-old Savilian Professor of Astronomy, but the better for this. Wren's greatness lay in realizing grand possibilities. A reverie over Serlio's reconstructions of the Roman Theatre of Marcellus was his starting point, and Oxford, in its first flush of Augustan grandeur, was to have its own morsel of Rome, complete with banked seats and a curved auditorium facing the great south door whence the academic actors make their entrance. And, yes, to finish off the illusion, above our heads a *velarium*, the roped awning over the classical theatre, pulled back to show Robert Streeter's *Religion, Arts and Science triumphing over Envy, Hate and Malice*.

The fancy is complete and the Act, now known as Encaenia, can begin, with the doctors and proctors in their statutable habits, the Passmore Edwards and Newdigate Prize winners spouting Latin and English verses, the eminent and meritorious hailed by the Public Orator in Latin (trans-lations provided). Has the Chancellor forgotten his spectacles? In earlier ages this would scarcely have escaped the notice of Terrae Filius, the licensed fool whose job it was to make fun of the proceedings, and whose coarseness embraced the entire university. At the great Act of 1733, for example, made memorable by the performances of 'one Handel and his lousy crew of foreign fiddlers', the fellows of St John's were called 'Jacobite Topers', those of All Souls were said to have 'debauch'd more Girls than they have read Books' and the Chancellor was saluted with 'Hail mitred Hog!' Somewhere among Encaenia's audience even now there may be somebody who yearns to echo the anonymous clown by crying out to the university assembled: '. . . I believe most of you profess more than you practise, whether you have taken any Degree or no Degree, tho' a very small *Degree* of Goodness I fear is to be found amongst you all . . .'

The High Street

Dusty, clamorous, rugged and intransigent, the High Street flourishes Oxford's eternally uneasy synthesis in the face of the traveller. Along its epic curve from Carfax in the west to Magdalen in the east, city and university both meet and shun each other, and among the sellers of fancy waistcoats and snuff for undergraduate poseurs, wines a touch more recherché than those in college cellars, and siren inducements to Long Vacation wanderings in quest of penniless romance, the noblest of its towers, porches and gables seem like the emplacements of an occupying power. There is an insolent grandeur in the arcaded screen of the Queen's College (as impenetrable nowadays as any Forbidden City) with Queen Caroline under her dome calmly disregarding an aggressive fist from Anne in her niche on the other side of the street; the plain gabled sweep of University College, and the grim neo-Jacobean of Oriel's Rhodes Building make up a vista of uncompromising gestures, a perpetual challenge to the chafing independence of the town.

Now and then the citizens strike back, and in the tense air of roistering Saturday nights during term time we catch an echo of that most famous of all battles in the High, the riot of 1355, taking place with sinister irony on 4th February, the feast of Saint Scholastica. Crying 'Slay, Slay, Havoc, Havoc, Smight fast, Give good knocks!' Oxford let itself go with blind rage upon the gownsmen, killing, maiming, plundering and destroying so completely from sunrise to afternoon that 'our mother the University . . . which had but two days before many sons, was now almost foresaken and left forlorn.'

Not for long. As though in everlasting atonement, the street's eastern end enshrines a yearly rite of exclusively academic sadness, when on June days outside Sir Thomas Jackson's Examination Schools, a yellow Elizabethan country house of 1884, undergraduates celebrate their final papers in libations of Veuve Clicquot and *méthode champenoise*. Armatures and ligaments of wire, a litter of green glass, plump corks like Palaeolithic fertility figures and maps of alcohol on the pavement mark the beginnings of responsibility, worry and guilt. Amid the stately mockery of the High's *mise-en-scène* Oxford ends.

Trinity

Trinity's charm lies in the simple fact that it has never pretended to be anything special. Your classic Trinity man is the Oxonian archetype, friendly, easy-going, fanciful, rather idle, with a touch of the eccentric but nothing of the poseur, steadily holding to the middle of whatever road he chooses to travel. Over the wall to the north is St John's, wealthy and High Tory, drinking deep to Charles the Martyr, by whose Archbishop Laud it was made an academic Something. To the west, with a hideous, candy-striped Butterfield chapel rudely getting its oar in, is Trinity's traditional rival, Balliol, the college with the dullest buildings in the university and the only one to transplant the humourless fervour of Cambridge to its pursuit of High Seriousness. Between these two Oxford extremes Trinity spreads its sublime vistas – Wren and Townesend's Garden Quad seen at its best as a screen against sloping sunlight across broad lawns, the neo-classical library viewed through the lime walks where Charles I's courtiers took their ease during the days of waiting and hoping in the Civil War, and the prospect from the head of the Turl down across the Broad and through the wrought-iron gates to the unmatched handsomeness of true English Baroque in the chapel.

Who could envisage, in such relaxed beauty, a setting for one of the sharpest convulsions in England's Christian history, the Anglican revival leading to the momentous Roman apostasy of Trinity's own cardinal, John Henry Newman? Yet, in true Trinity style, we find him writing excitedly of college dinners off 'fish, flesh and fowl, beautiful salmon, haunches of mutton, lamb etc., fine strong beer, served up in old pewter plates and misshapen earthenware jugs. Tell Mamma there were gooseberry, raspberry and apricot pies. And in all this the joint did not go round, but there was such a profusion that scarcely two ate of the same.' St Peter's dream? Perhaps after all the Trinity of those days, its scholars 'distinguished by singular purity and simplicity of life, by a very high standard of religious thought and feeling', their ethos 'a combination of manliness and gentleness', was the right place for spiritual romance. Those deep perspectives, the chapel gorgeous and Italianate, perhaps even a recollection of the 'monkish dog-kennels' on which the college was founded, must all have played their part. No wonder Arthur Hugh Clough, looking over the wall from ascetic Balliol, pined for the talk 'at Trinity wines about Gothic buildings and Beauty'.

The University Museum

North Oxford is a palimpsest of Victorian idealism, written over, and happily not always rubbed out, by visionaries and philanthropists. This is the domain of the women's colleges; Somerville, scornfully brilliant, St Anne's and St Hugh's, lively, contentious and political, and Lady Margaret Hall, where, in the days before men were admitted to the foundation, undergraduates were the most *mondaine* and fashion-conscious in the university. It is the realm, too, of 'the Parks-system', handsome houses in leafy avenues built for 19th-century dons free at last to marry and create the North Oxford world of 'domestic hearths, afternoon teas, and perambulators', shopping in North Parade, and worshipping at 'Pip & Jim', G. E. Street's aggressively consequential church of St Philip and St James.

The zone, then, of Good Intentions, symbolized at their purest by the University Museum, intended to assemble 'all the materials explanatory of the organic beings placed upon the globe' and designed by Benjamin Woodward, but forever associated with the guiding spirit of the enterprise, John Ruskin. He wanted, and got for a time at least, the energies of the unskilled workman, whose natural impulse towards creating beauty was to be fostered by morning prayers and the spirit of primitive socialism which Ruskin's ideas instilled.

It was, perhaps, just a little too grand to be sustained, either by its creators or by the University itself. The façade was never properly finished, and Hippolyte Taine, disgusted by its 'staring brick, with pointed roof and ugly little cupolas like extinguishers', concluded that Ruskin's books were better than his buildings. Nothing, however, quite prepares us for the stupendous interior, part railway terminus, part Crystal Palace, part Victorian tea-garden, with its palm branches of wrought iron and glass roof sheltering, among other exhibits, the remains of a dodo.

The explanatory materials and organic beings are not all here – did anybody ever suppose they would be, in the city where T. E. Huxley had trounced Bishop Wilberforce in the famous debate on Darwin's revolutionary theories? As if to prove the world's immensity, behind the museum itself lies an Oxford particular, the uniquely absorbing Pitt Rivers ethnographical collection, case upon case of grotesque, beautiful and sinister human artefacts reflecting scenes, faces and activities which Ruskin perhaps all too seldom contemplated.

The Holywell Music Room

Music, like God, is ubiquitous in Oxford: at its grandest in the Sheldonian or Town Hall concerts, or in the daily choral offices of Christ Church, New College and Magdalen, at its loudest in the thump of the disco beat wafting out towards Iffley, Marston and Cumnor from a summer commem. ball, at its most intimate in the rehearsals of a fledgling string quartet or a trickle of piano notes heard through an open window in some narrow lane off the High.

18th-century Oxonians so loved their concerts that they built a special saloon to house them, a plain-fronted hall as discreet as any dissenting chapel, set demurely back off the street behind Wadham College and known as the Holywell Music Room. With its 'Orchestre' and 'elegant Stucco-work in the Cieling' and 'two very handsome Lustres of Cut Glass, for which we are indebted to the Ladies: who raised a Subscription of 66l. 13s. 6d. for that Purpose' it opened on 9th July, 1748, with a performance of Handel's oratorio *Esther*, and for the next hundred years welcomed all the finest European performers. The adored Mrs Billington, whom Haydn called '*eine grosses Genie*', warbled opera airs, Fischer and Abel played the oboe and viola da gamba to a miracle, and the last of the great male sopranos, Tenducci, for whom Mozart composed and who, so Casanova tells us, fathered two children, and Marchesi, who had himself castrated to become the star singer of the age, perpetrated prodigies befitting their nature.

The end, when it came, was in a burst of vocal fireworks. To the echoes of Maria Caterina Rosalbina Caradori Allan (née de Munck – born Milan, died Surbiton) whom Mendelssohn called 'so pretty, so pleasing, so elegant . . . so heartless, so unintelligent, so soulless', Angelica Catalani, who had charmed Napoleon and the Prince Regent and bequeathed her larynx to the University of Bologna, and the matchless Giuditta Pasta, creator of the heroines of Bellini and Donizetti, the Holywell Music Room closed its doors. Only in 1901, when English musical life was renewing itself after prolonged dreams of interminable oratorio, were they opened once more – for Oxford, as loud after all with bells as Venice or Rome, had found it could not endure silence for very long.

The Bodleian Library

'The fourth and last day (30 Aug.) the King, Prince and Court went to the publick Library, newly restored by Sir Thomas Bodley, consisting then only of the middle part that now is erected by the benefaction of Duke Humphrey and others: there he spent at least an hour, took into his hands several books, perused and gave his learned censure of them.' A remarkable thing, doubtless, for a mere English monarch to do, but he was that royal Scottish scribbler King James I, who now sits enthroned under his motto *Beati Pacifici* in the Schools Quadrangle of the Bodleian Library.

It is not his foundation, of course, any more than Jesus College is Queen Elizabeth's or the Queen's is Queen Philippa's, though both women are similarly honoured. Nor is it William Herbert, Earl of Pembroke's, whose statue, based by Hubert Le Sueur on a Rubens portrait, looks towards the King from the west end of the gloomy courtyard, a 'valley of the shadow of books', like some forgotten monument from which the desert sand has just blown away. Second largest library in England, its readers fed from a stock of 3,000,000 volumes and 50,000 manuscripts, the Bodleian was created from a small mediaeval collection founded by Henry V's ill-fated brother Duke Humphrey of Gloucester and renewed by the Elizabethan scholar and diplomat Sir Thomas Bodley, who arranged that every officially registered book printed in England should be given to the library.

Thus the books are siphoned beneath Oxford's very soil in tunnelled vaults, like blood to a body, and, in the reading rooms above, the studious, the plodding, the *dilettanti* and the desperate wait for their little green slips to be transmogrified into *The Hog Hath Lost His Pearl*, *Jane's Fighting Ships vol ii*, *A Grammar of Modern Coptic* or *The Naughtiest Girl in the School*. While they wait, they can browse through the latest editions of *Acta Musicologica*, *Notes & Queries* or *Analecta Bollandiana*, or pick a name from the Danish *Who's Who* or the *Bottin Mondain*, or look up their great-grandfathers in old copies of the University Calendar.

And when it arrives at last? The Lower Reading Room, with its classicists and theologians, will settle intently to work; the Camera, in its darkened bays, will look at it quizzically, unopened on the desk; Duke Humphrey's, most seductive of all, will carry it away with an enigmatic smile to an eyrie in the balconies at its western end. As for the Upper Reading Room, its readers look, not at books but at one another, in expressions of beautiful hopelessness, their rows of heads going up like a windswept field as Someone passes, adored, loathed, desired or mysterious, along its bright galleries.

Magdalen

Rich young rulers go to Christ Church, revolutionaries to Balliol, reactionaries to St John's, Welshmen to Jesus and northern men to the Queen's. At 17th-century Wadham, Oliver Cromwell's brother-in-law Warden Wilkins fostered the circle of free enquirers into science and technology which later became the Royal Society. At Corpus a swarm of bees gathering annually in the front quad till they were driven away by the Parliamentarians in 1648 symbolized the 'hive' imagined by the founder in his statutes, where 'ingenious bees' were to make 'wax and honey to God's honour, night and day'; and still do so, judging by the annual proportion of first class degrees.

But Magdalen, set apart from the others on the eastern edge of the old city walls, has always been superbly different. Style and singularity, a resolute distinctiveness, have marked it from the beginning. Its sympathies were emphatically Puritan, for example, when other colleges were Royalist, and an annual dinner commemorates its countercheck to royal bullying by James II in 1686. He was a king without imagination, and Magdalen has no time for the unimaginative.

Its very stones tell us so. Whim and fantasy have spread them out in haphazard nonchalance among the gardens and water-walks. No quadrangles, of course, Magdalen studiously avoids that, but, for perversity's sake, a triangle south of the chapel, and, across the croquet lawns, an arcaded rococo palace still known as New Buildings. Beneath its back windows fallow deer rut, shed their velvet, and nibble port-soaked sugar-lumps tossed to them from the panneled rooms, shaded by trees whose roots are nourished on the bones of their primitive ancestors, mammoths' tusks and the British bear *Ursus Anglicus*.

Above all else the tower, begun in 1492, embodies Magdalen's particularity. Where other Oxford towers are thick fists clenched ready for defence, this, a slender campanile with no obvious relation to the chapel close by, is a long, taper-fingered hand drawing us winsomely yet ruthlessly across the bridge and into the city, or sending us out again with a benign valediction. From its roof, each first morning of May, the college choir sings the seventeenth-century hymn *Te Deum Patrem*, to which the junketing undergraduates beneath traditionally listen in vain, for the notes, floating upwards, are inaudible to any but God.

The Radcliffe Camera

Like the shrine of the oracle at Delphi or the temple of the sun at Cuzco, the Radcliffe Camera is the navel of the universe, a gigantic plug of English rococo thrust amid the Oxford colleges to hold them fast, yet, for all its allusions to classical Rome and Renaissance Italy, a building without a direct parallel in the architecture of the world. James Gibbs designed it in 1737, using an idea already mooted years earlier by Sir Christopher Wren in an unfulfilled project for a free-standing circular library, and backed by a bequest of £40,000 from the will of the philanthropic Dr John Radcliffe. Unusually in the annals of the period relations between architect and patrons were cordial to the last, and Gibbs praised the overseeing Trustees for their 'unanimity, integrity and candor, during the whole time I had the honour of serving you, from the laying the first stone of the fabrick to its finishing.'

It was his masterpiece and he knew it. As a former Catholic he was a natural favourite with ardently Jacobite Oxford, and it was in a scandalous flourish of treason and High Toryism that the Camera opened on 13th April, 1749. After degree ceremonies at the Sheldonian and the presentation of the doorkey by the Duke of Beaufort to the Vice-Chancellor, the distinguished company was treated to a speech by Dr King, Principal of St Mary's Hall (now part of Oriel) in which the word *Redeat* (may he return) introducing a vilification of the Hanoverians was repeated several times to remind the audience of Prince Charles Edward Stuart, whom they still hoped would come again to his inheritance.

Oxford burned with indignant pamphleteering, menaces and brawls, but the Camera endured, its lower bays remaining an open arcade until 1863, and its staircase and domed upper floor stuccoed and carved to lend an incongruous, not always merited grace to the plodding of scholars. A mausoleum of Augustan benevolence? A Jacobite ziggurat? Lit up at night, when it shows best of all, the Camera looks like some monstrous folly in a nobleman's park and we strain to hear the sounds of music and feasting from within. And at midnight, when all Oxford is abed, the heads of all the colleges sometimes tiptoe inside, the Vice-Chancellor cuts the guy-ropes which hold it down, and the great academic balloon sails gracefully upwards into the moonlight above the dark pinnacles for a Grand Metaphysical Outing.

All Souls

'The souls of all the faithful departed, and more especially those of Henry V, lately King of England and France, the Duke of Clarence, and the other lords and lieges of the realm of England whom the havoc of that warfare between the two realms hath drenched with the bowl of bitter death' – those at least were the objects of Archbishop Chichele's piety when, in 1438, he founded a college for a warden and forty fellows.

Fellows, that is the point, and has always been, to the exasperation of Oxford's critics. How can a foundation without undergraduates, without a student body of any sort whatever, justify its existence? All Souls has never sought to do so. It is, indeed, above recourse to such measures. If its clerks pray at all nowadays, it is not for the English dead of the battle of Agincourt, but that so hand-plucked a body of fellows, emeritus, by examination or otherwise, may be permitted to survive in an age which modishly decries élitism.

And what do the fellows do? Nothing, say the detractors – but then Oxford has always been accused of that, ever since and before Edward Gibbon wrote that 'I spent fourteen months at Magdalen College; they proved the fourteen months the most idle and unprofitable of my whole life', and Neubauer, the pioneer Hebrew scholar, told a French visitor ' no one really works here – five or six at most'. To provoke the doubters even further there is Hawksmoor's North Quad, that incomparably elegant fusion of native English romanticism and Augustan wit, a permanent setting for an academic opera, created through his subtle persuasion of the fellows that he was giving them 'antient durable Publick Buildings . . . instead of erecting new fantasticall,

perishable trash.' Can it be that in the Codrington Library, Gothic without, Venetian within, or under those confectionery towers, mocking the Wykehamist sobriety of New College nearby with their teasing sophistication, there is somebody actually working?

The answer, alas, is invariably yes. The *magnum mysterium* of All Souls, of which some of its own fellows are occasionally rather dubious, is to hide its true face behind a legendary mask of port and pomposity, dropped now and then to show us, in a weirdly Oxonian way, the secret reasons for its survival.

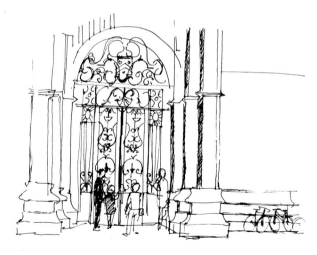

The Covered Market

Once there was Grimbly Hughes 'a household word in the district as symbolical of the very best in Provisions, Groceries, Confectionery, Wines, Spirits, Cigars etc.', there were Martyrs the Hairdressers, Lunn's for Meerschaum pipes, Fred G. Alden for 'Country House Electric Lighting, Heating, Pumping and Water Supply', Cooke's Yenidjeh Cigarettes at 10/6d per 100, breeches from Bartlett & Carter who 'respectfully sollicit your Patronage', Nicholl's Quality Footwear 'agents for Waukeezi, Tru Phit, Gradua and Diana brands', Walker's Plus Four Suits from 6 guineas, the Shamrock Tea Rooms, featuring 'the Yeats room, formerly the dining room of the Poet' and 'a bastion of the Old City Wall in the Tea Garden', Macpherson's Garage selling 'Austin Landaulettes, roomy, smart and speedy' and the Oxford Wireless Telephone Co. Ltd. – 'our staff consists of ex-Royal Navy wireless officers and mechanics' – with its stock of Gecophones, Artistophones, Marconiphones and the Polar Receiver.

All gone, of course: 'all changed, changed utterly' as Yeats may or may not have muttered over his Shamrock dinner under the bastion of the city wall. The days of the obsequious city shopkeeper, stifling a curse as he bowed to a Gentleman Commoner or the Warden of a college, have vanished, but the wondrous Covered Market abides, a Levantine bazaar of purveyors to dons' wives in search of sharper flavours to tickle dulled North Oxford palates, and hucksters peddling everything from birdseed to *baguettes*. Outside the butcher's, above drifts of bloodsoaked sawdust, hangs a whole goat, a hare like a racing greyhound or a turkey as big as a dodo. In the grocer's, high over the regiments of Earl Grey and the glistening carboys of pickled pawpaws, are vague, dusty canisters of Something which has been there for such a very long time that an act of faith decrees that it remain unexamined. One day perhaps, a foolhardy shopgirl, abseiling the shelves, will lift the lid and not only she and the Stilton and fig-seasoned coffee will vanish, but all the Covered Market together, taking with it the cut-price jeans, the dog biscuits, the secondhand records, the mangetout peas and the tables at Brown's and George's where the undergraduates gnawing bacon sandwiches are less likely to be discussing Hegel than each other.

Saint Mary's Church

Climb to the top of St Mary's tower, built at the end of the 13th century, and look out over Oxford. A stone text, whose allusions and annotations all point towards an ineluctable theme. For, abandoned though it now appears to a godless world, its shape, its rhetoric, its musculature and bone structure are those of religion, a mineral element in the soil and water of the city. Oxford, in its secret, confused, wild English way, tends instinctively towards the spiritual, and the University Church of St Mary concentrates this enduring experience as a potent emblem.

It succeeds triumphantly in being several things at once. The noblest statement of pure Gothic in Oxford, it was raised over two mediaeval centuries to culminate in an exuberant blossoming of ballflower crockets and the tall, broad lantern windows of English Perpendicular. In such a guise it stands as the parent, dignified and authoritative, of the Bodleian Library's functional elegance, the farmhouse cosiness of Brasenose College and the wonderful delinquent fantasies of Hawksmoor's North Quad of All Souls, Oxford's last fling with the style it loved best.

For a time St Mary's was the university itself, when the Congregation House on its north side held the library created by Thomas de Cobham, Bishop of Worcester, and witnessed the creation of degrees, and the Chancellor's Court nearby regulated the discipline of scholars and citizens alike. But, more significantly than this, the building was a theatre for those restless convulsions of dogma, doubt and heresy which mark England's bizarre relationship with Christianity. Here Wycliffe's Lollard followers barred the doors against Archbishop Arundel. Here Cranmer, Ridley and Latimer committed themselves to Protestant martyrdom, John

Wesley castigated the lackadaisical Augustan clergy 'and having insulted and abus'd all Degrees, from the highest to the lowest, was in a manner hissed out of the Pulpit by the lads', and here John Henry Newman, 'breaking the silence with words and thoughts which were a religious movement, subtle, sweet, mournful' changed the character of Anglican worship for ever. Even the porch, Nicholas Stone's superbly shameless morsel of Italian Baroque complete with Virgin and Child, tacked on to the Gothic harmonies in 1637 under Archbishop Laud's patronage, has its meaning in the context of Oxford's abidingly awkward and intense religiosity.

Folded into a druidical mist, viewed from a sodden hillside through a screen of dripping branches, seen against a clear dawn, its towers like diacritical marks upon the lines of a text, or coyly changing its colours as evening comes on, Oxford beheld from a distance is as elusive and capricious as it was when we were there within it. Matthew Arnold spoke of it, twice and memorably, as dreaming, but the only reveries were Arnold's, those of a flesh-and-blood Oxonian eternally lacing his quest for gravity with delicious in-ventions. Oxford never dreams, it is far too wakeful and predatory, too eager to take us for its own. Turning to look back from Cumnor or Iffley or as the Paddington train pulls out, each of us reads the chosen signals. A warning? An insult? An invitation or an embrace?